MW01485953

The Scholarship & College Essay Planning Kit

The

Scholarship & College

Essay Planning Kit

A Guide for Uneasy Student Writers

Marianne Ragins

TSW Publishing
P. O. Box 176
Centreville, Virginia 20122
www.scholarshipworkshop.com
TSW Publishing is a division of The Scholarship Workshop LLC

The Scholarship & College Essay Planning Kit was written to
provide accurate advice to readers. Neither the author, the
publisher, nor any entity associated with *The Scholarship &
College Essay Planning Kit* assume any liability for errors,
omissions, or inaccuracies. Any action you take or do not take as
a result of reading *The Scholarship & College Essay Planning Kit*
is entirely your responsibility.

ISBN: 978-0-9767660-6-3

Printed in the United States of America

This book is available at special quantity discounts for bulk
purchases for sales promotions, premiums, fundraising, and
educational use. Special versions or book excerpts can also be
created to fit specific needs. For more information, please contact
info@scholarshipworkshop.com or call 703 579-4245. You can
also write: TSW Publishing, P. O. Box 176, Centreville, Virginia
20122.

Dedication

To my mother, Laura; my husband, Ivan; and my little ones, Aria and Cameron; your love, motivation, and presence in my life keep me going.

For Gloria Laverne Solomon, Sammie L. Moore Sr. and Dr. Angela E. Grant

As people who truly got the most from life and helped us to get the most from ours, your sunny smiles, loving hearts and generous ways will be remembered forever by all of your family and friends.

CONTENTS

INTRODUCTION

The Scholarship & College Essay Planning Kit is an essential resource for students who prefer not to write essays, but still need to do so. If you use the tools included in this kit, you *can* complete an essay for a scholarship program, college, or university even if writing is not your favorite task.

The first toolkit includes the planning essentials. It helps you with steps to take before you write. It also helps you formulate ideas and gives you an easy outline format for putting together your essay.

The next toolkit focuses on helping you write about certain topics including yourself, your extracurricular activities, your future career goals and helping you answer specific essay questions. This section also includes several essay examples to show you how to use the outline format for *your* essay.

Additional toolkit sections include those to help you organize your essay, decide the most important elements to include for maximum impact, and how to proofread and polish your essay to help you stand out in a crowd of other applicants.

Finally, the essay kit includes ways to determine your own essay topic if you're given the option to do so, and a list of some of the most common essay prompts and questions you may need to answer. A list of transition words to help your essay flow better and a summary of do's and don'ts are also included to help you get your essay written successfully.

THE PLANNING TOOLS

Before You Write

Wondering what to do before you write? A good idea would be to complete the following activities before putting pen to paper.

Finish your résumé/activity list if you haven't already. Refer to the chapter, Writing Your Scholarship Résumé: How to Stand Out and Why Grades Don't Mean Everything," in *Winning Scholarships for College* for more information.

Research the organization or company sponsoring the scholarship or award.

Learn why the scholarship was established and the mission of the organization. If one or more of your activities fits the reasoning behind why the scholarship was established or the organization's mission you may want to highlight this in your essay.

Understand the question. Think of several ways you might answer and write them down.

Look at the scholarship application. What do most of the questions focus on: academics, community involvement, or unique experiences? If an organization asks most of its application questions about community involvement, then try to build your essay around activities you do that benefit the community.

Now that you've done some preliminary work, spend ten minutes jotting down ideas. Write about whatever comes to mind as you think about the organization, the scholarship, the question, and you. Don't worry about grammar, structure, or spelling. Just write! It's very important to get your initial thoughts down on paper. These could be your most creative and unique.

For writing essays I have found that the basic five-paragraph essay format is an easy one to use. For example, here is a simple outline for an essay that can be jazzed up with unique variations.

Easy Outline for General Essay Format

I.   Introduction - One paragraph

    A. Use a quotation, poem, thought, amazing fact, idea, question, or simple statement to draw your reader into your topic.

    B. The main idea does not have to be stated in the first sentence, but it should definitely lead to and be related to your main idea or thesis statement, which should introduce three main points you will develop in the body of your essay.

    C. Avoid using statements such as, "I am going to talk about . . . " or "This essay is about . . . "

II.   Body - Three paragraphs

    A. Support the main idea with facts, thoughts, ideas, published poetry, quotes, and other intriguing, insightful material that will captivate your audience.

B. Present clear images.

C. If necessary, use a thesaurus to ensure that you are not using the same words repeatedly. Using a word over and over will become monotonous for your audience and distract them from your subject.

III. Conclusion - One paragraph

A. Restate the main idea in an original way.

B. You can again use a poem or quotation to leave an impression. However, avoid using this tactic in all three parts of the essay. It may appear repetitious and unoriginal.

C. Refer to the future in terms of your plans pertaining to the subject of your essay. For example, in an essay describing your future career goals, refer to yourself in the career that you have outlined. This reference should project you, and the ideas you presented in the essay, into the future. Refer to the last paragraphs of the three sample essays for an illustration.

Special Note - Using quotations or poems shows that you are well read and imaginative. Be selective and look for quotes that are enlightening and profound.

THE WRITING TOOLS

Writing a Basic Essay About Yourself

In order to write a basic essay about yourself, you must complete your résumé or list of activities first, as mentioned in the planning tools. This résumé will be a very important resource when writing your essay. We'll get to actually writing and putting your essay together in the organizer tools section. But first, let's start with the basics.

Think of three adjectives or words that describe you. Look at your résumé or activity list. Do any adjectives or nouns come to mind? To get different points of view, ask a friend or a relative what adjectives or nouns they would use to describe you.

Examples

Creative
Enthusiastic
Dependable
Leader
Dreamer
Compassionate

Aggressive
Motivated
Determined
Responsible
Curious
Energetic
Active
Explorer
Organizer
Diverse
Seeker
Competitive
Innovative
Intelligent
Confident
Socially conscious
Well-rounded
Philosopher

Once you've finished and have at least three good adjectives or nouns that fit you perfectly, start to group activities that correspond with each adjective or noun. Before doing this make sure you are clear on the definitions of those you've chosen. For example, let's pick confident. The definition of confident, according to *Webster's New World Dictionary*, "is someone who is assured; certain; sure of one self."

Activities for confident might be:
- Debate Team
- Literary Team
- Student Council
- Mock Trial Team

Activities for socially conscious or compassionate might be:
- Church Youth Group
- Red Cross Volunteer
- Toys for Tots Volunteer
- Habitat for Humanity Volunteer

Activities for energetic might be:
- Softball Team
- Track Team
- Spirit or Pep Club
- Varsity Cheerleader

Activities for leader might be:
- President, Spanish Club
- Treasurer, Student Council

- Assistant Editor, School Newspaper
- Shift Leader or Assistant Manager, Part-time Job

You could also describe yourself as enlightened. For this adjective your activities might be:
- Participant, Summer Youth Group – Young Entrepreneurs Council
- Early Scholar Program at local university taking courses in World History and Psychology

When describing yourself in an essay, select three adjectives or words that characterize you or your values and support them by telling why these adjectives fit you and your attitude about life. These adjectives will make up the body of your essay and should be used as overall guidelines to provide unity and cohesiveness.

As you elaborate on the descriptive adjectives or words you have chosen, strive to show the following qualities in your essay:

Sense of responsibility— Demonstrate your sense of responsibility and diligence. You might convey this by your involvement in extracurricular activities or through academic achievements.

Participation in extracurricular activities— In the community and your high school, your out- of- school activities should exhibit initiative, leadership skills, and enthusiasm. It is a good idea to have your résumé handy as you write your essays. One of the best ways to stand out from other scholarship applicants is through your activities and personal experiences.

Your potential for growth— Show how you have grown as a person from participation in extracurricular activities and how your growth could be an asset to the college or university you attend or would like to attend and to your community.

These qualities should be evident in every essay you write. Even if the essay is not a descriptive personal essay, it is still important to show your connection to these qualities.

A Descriptive Essay Reworked

The following essay is an example of a descriptive essay written by young lady. The first example has not been revised. The second example is improved with specific references, more details, and corrections.

Unrevised Essay

From a young age, i was diagnosed with ADHD and a speech disorder. I have a difficult time decoding words and pronouncing some letter sounds. Because of my speech, it made it hard for me in school. In English and history classes, i have a hard time with reading the textbook and doing presentations. Moreover, because i have a hard time with the English language, i have a harder time with learning other languages. Even though this causes me to have a setback in my education, i try to work hard on my schoolwork.

Revised Essay

At a young age, 6, I was diagnosed with Attention Deficit Hyperactivity Disorder (ADHD) and Phonological Processing Disorder. More specifically, Phonological Processing Disorder is a speech disorder that has always made it difficult to decode words and pronounce some letter sounds such as "s," "l: and "r". As a result, excelling in school has been a challenge. For example, in English and history classes, it is challenging to read the textbook and conduct presentations. Imagine striving for a high GPA with these problems! Moreover, because I have a tough time with the English language, I have an even harder time with other languages such as Mandarin Chinese which I tried anyway. I want to overcome my disability and not let it overcome me. Even though my issues are extremely challenging, I continue to strive for the best. Despite my hardships, I have a 3.14

GPA and have taken several AP courses including history which required reading and oral presentations. In addition, I have involved myself in numerous charitable activities for more than half my life. These activities, such as being a teacher for 3 to 4 year olds at XYZ Baptist Church in Example, Virginia; and being a member of the Red Cross Youth team force me out of my comfort zone and allow me to work on overcoming my obstacles while at the same time serving my community in a positive manner

WRITING ABOUT YOUR ACTIVITIES

If you completed the first section of the writing tools, you should now have at least three adjectives that describe you and your activities. Along with the adjectives you should also have a few specific extracurricular or community activities associated with each of them. If you've done that, you're now ready to give your essay

some character by writing about your activities and not just listing them as you did in the previous section. It doesn't matter what your topic is, one of the best ways to make your essay unique and personal is to write about your activities and interests.

So how do you write about an activity and make it come alive for your readers? Think of your activities with these questions in mind:

Who?

- Who does the activity benefit?
- Does the activity benefit others? Is it for your school or your community? Is it for your church or the local Red Cross?

What?

- What is the activity?

If you are president or member of a club, give more than the name. Tell the readers what the activity involves. For example, one scholarship applicant wrote, "This year, I am president of the Junior Civitan Club. In the Junior Civitan Club, our responsibility is to serve our community. We have fed and clothed the homeless people in Birmingham, Alabama. We have also cleaned our nearby city park, and raised money for a scholarship for a student at our school." This applicant included not only specific information about the activity (What?), she also included who it benefited and where the activities associated with the Junior Civitan Club were conducted. She could also have included how the selfless acts she was doing now were a reflection of her desire to become a doctor (Why?). In addition, she could have discussed how she spent every Saturday morning for a month being involved in activities for the Junior Civitan Club (When?).

When?

- When do you participate in this activity?
- Is it after school, Saturday mornings, during the summer, before school, or some other time?

Where?

- Where do you participate in this activity?
- Is it something you do at school, in the city, at church, at the Chamber of Commerce, at your local hospital or newspaper, in a nearby city, at your state capitol, or somewhere else?

How?

- How does this activity benefit you or others?
- Does it benefit you? If it does, how so? Is it an incredible learning experience you can use to help you in your future career as an engineer, marketing executive, or a doctor? Is it helping you to apply principles you've learned in a class? How will you use the knowledge you gain to help others?
- Does it benefit others? How? Does your volunteering at a shelter provide nourishing food for the homeless? Does your singing in a choir at a senior citizen's home help to uplift and motivate those who listen?

Why?

- Why are you involved in the activity?
- Does it make you feel proud, helpful, or fulfilled? Is it preparing you for the future? For example, if you are a member of the Future Business Leaders of America (FBLA), is your involvement helping to prepare you for a career as an entrepreneur or an

executive? Or, as a debate team member, will you use the skills you gain as a politician or lawyer one-day?

WRITING ABOUT YOUR FUTURE CAREER GOALS

Need to know how to start an essay about your future career goals? You can use the same type of method used for writing about yourself. Write down your future career goals. Then write down the activities that relate to the goals or have prepared you for your goals. For example, my career goal was to be involved in journalism and communications as an adult. In the introduction of my essay, I began describing an interest in these areas that started in elementary school, continued into middle school, and increased in high school. I wrote the next three paragraphs on my activities in elementary, middle, and high school (complete essay at the end of this chapter).

You can also begin an essay about future career goals by writing that your interest in becoming a doctor, for example, stems from your efforts to be a responsible, self-

motivated, and compassionate young adult.
You could then reuse some of your essay
describing yourself (if you used these
adjectives) as part of your essay about your
future career goals. Make sure when doing
this you explain why you are so interested in
the career. For example, your interest in
being a doctor could have come from living
through the deaths of your brother and sister
who both had a hereditary disease that
skipped you.

An Essay Example from the Author

Future Career Goals

I wrote this essay at the beginning of my
scholarship quest. The requirements were to
write an essay about my future career goals
in relation to a journalism scholarship. The
essay revolves around my interest in
journalism and describes chronologically
how that interest blossomed from early
childhood into my young adult years. Clear,
original images are presented to reflect my
love of journalism. In the conclusion I refer to

the future in conjunction with my personal plans and ideals. For variety I added one additional paragraph.

I. Introduction

[1]**Throughout my life, I have been involved in many unique activities, many of which have been oriented in the area of communications and journalism.**[2] Therefore at an early age, I began to develop a desire to pursue a career in one or both of these fields. This desire has progressed from elementary and middle schools into high school. Anchored to a foundation formed over a span of many years, its roots are now unshakable.

1. This is the introductory paragraph. I used this paragraph to introduce the main idea of the essay, the development of my interest in communications and journalism throughout my school career.
2. The sentence in bold print is phrased as a simple statement to lead the reader into the essay.

II. Body

[3]The **building blocks of this foundation were laid**[4] in sixth grade when I began to participate in a weekly telecast at Walter P. Jones elementary school. **As the primary newscaster as well as the student who compiled all the stories for the Jones elementary news broadcast, I was fascinated by my work. It was challenging and exciting.**[5] As a result, while standing in front of a video camcorder, my **passion for journalism and communications**[6] began. Throughout that year I participated in essay and oratorical contests, debates, and plays. My desire had taken firm root.

3. Supporting paragraph. It shows the development and origin of my interest in journalism and communications.
4. Imagery – Creates an image in the mind of the reader.
5. Presents facts to support the development of my interest. It also gives evidence of my responsibility and enthusiasm for my work. I point

out specific activities I have participated in that support the main idea.

6. Word choice variety – I could have said, "my *interest* in journalism and communications began." Passion sounded more exciting and is apt to grab the reader's attention.

[7]Furthermore, in middle school I continued to compete in many contests involving these areas of interest. **The winning oration that I had written for the Optimist International Oratorical Contest (District Level) I recited along with several others on Channel 6, here in Macon, Georgia.**[8]**The seedlings of journalistic youth that had been planted in elementary school were mushrooming into boisterous young children of communicative creativity.**[9] This **quote by the English essayist Joseph Addison aptly described my feelings then and still does now. "Words, when well-chosen and presented, have so great a force in them, that a description often**

gives us more lively ideas than the sights of the things themselves."[10]

7. Supporting paragraph.
8. Presentation of fact. Once again I used specific activities and honors from my résumé to support the main idea.
9. Imagery.
10. Quote.

[11]As I progressed into my ninth-grade year in school, my interest in journalism and communication intensified. **Northeast High School encompassed a much broader scope than middle school because it contained the *Salmagundi* literary magazine, the *Golden Star* newspaper, and the *Valhalla* yearbook, which helped me gain more experience in journalism as I became actively involved with an actual publication.[12] The children of communicative creativity had now become young adults of journalistic potential.[13]**

11. Supporting paragraph. Outlines the progression of my interests into high school.
12. Fact. This statement shows my potential for growth in this area and that I was aware of that growth. Here, I have also used activities from my résumé to help illustrate my point.
13. Imagery.

III. Conclusion

[14]**I would like to pursue a career in journalism and/or communications because both areas, which are closely interrelated, have become an essential part of my life. Over the years this desire has grown like a sturdy young plant preparing to take over the world or me (whichever comes first).**[15] To me, communication is a marvel because it can open doors into worlds otherwise unknown. **Communication can transport you to the tombs of Egypt, the gold of Africa, or the green hills of Ireland.**[16] Through the power of words, spoken or

read, man possesses the ability to convey anything.

> 14. The first two sentences restate the main idea and form the beginning of the conclusion.
> 15. Imagery.
> 16. Imagery.

[17]All of my experiences in writing and speaking have helped me to see the importance of communication; for example, in the field of broadcasting where the presentation of information can influence and motivate. As a child, people and their attitudes provoked curiosity within my young mind. As a young adult, people, their attitudes, and their effect on our changing world fascinate me. Journalism and communications embrace both my curiosity as a child and my fascination as a young adult. **A career in either area would not only satisfy my goals but would hopefully make me an asset to my community, state, and eventually the world.**[18]

17. Displays my growth in this area and my potential for future growth.
18. This statement exhibits my commitment to improving the society in which I live and it refers to the future.

A Great Essay Example from a Student

Future Career Goals

The following essay was written by a student for the Ragins/Braswell National scholarship program, which she subsequently won. This student pulled us into her essay in the first sentence by stating a shocking fact about her brother (underlined). She then proceeds to do a wonderful job of weaving extracurricular activities (underlined) into her essay to illustrate her points. Throughout her paragraphs, she refers to how she can positively affect the future in her community (underlined). Transition words (bold) are also used to help her essay flow easily from one thought to another.

> *<u>In 2011, my younger brother committed suicide at age 16 due to untreated mental illness</u>. **As a result**, it is my hope to make a difference in the lives of young African-American children with mental disorders that may not receive the treatment they need due to cultural stigmas and lack of*

*understanding. **As** a future occupational therapist, <u>I plan to be a catalyst for change in the mental health of the African-American community.</u> <u>It is my hope to work with youth **and** their families in at-risk, urban communities to educate and empower people to care for their mental health. My vision is to work with children with mental disorders, developmental disabilities, and autism.</u> My background of working with youth with disabilities, serving urban communities, and engaging in diverse cultures has helped prepare me for this challenge. A Master's degree in Occupational Therapy will guide me through my career as I assist children in urban areas to develop and recover skills essential to their mental and physical well-being. **As** an occupational therapist, I can lead them through practical solutions such as adapting the environment, teaching useful skills **and** engaging in activities that work toward treatment goals.*

***Throughout** my college and post-undergraduate career, I have cultivated a passion for helping people in urban and* *economically disadvantaged communities. My bachelor's degree in cultural anthropology and sociology provided me with a solid understanding of social factors that can prevent people from getting the help they desperately need. <u>I studied in an immersion program in South Africa</u> and gained a better understanding of the cultural and economic contributors that prevent people in poverty from receiving treatment. <u>**Upon** graduation, I worked as Therapeutic Staff Support for children at a low- income school in West Philadelphia, giving me experience working with children with mental disorders. My experience working in fundraising and community engagement with United Way,</u> has given me a broader perspective for how a community's needs can determine an individual's needs. I am **now** prepared to take the broad vision I gained on social issues and apply my knowledge to helping one individual at a time through occupational therapy.*

In this new career, <u>I hope to be a part of destigmatizing mental disorders in the</u>

<u>African American community through my</u>
*<u>skill set and experience</u>. I am ready **now***
more than ever to make the critical
changes our community needs for a
healthier and well- balanced future.

Essay Example from a Student

Future Career Goals

This is an example of an essay in need of additional details to illustrate the student's points. The essay includes many general statements that could apply to any student, **not just** the student who wrote the essay. This student should have included certain activities from their résumé to define and shape the essay and also help it come alive for readers. Additional details and activities will also provide a basis for why the student wants to pursue the career choice mentioned in the essay.

Although the student did include a quote, they should have researched it to use it correctly and include its source. Using quoteland.com, the student might have found that this phrase is actually a Chinese proverb that states, "Give a man a fish and he will eat for a day. Teach a man to fish and he will eat for the rest of his life." Appropriately citing the quote in the student's essay example that follows would have helped the statement and its meaning be more powerful within the context of the essay particularly if this student had associated the quote with an extracurricular activity in which they participated or some other detail from their lives to which the quote could be related.

I plan to earn a major in Business Administration and Accounting, while minoring in Finance and Music. I will use my experience from this to help others with many genres. I could help with their taxes and teach them how to do their own taxes. Like the saying goes, "Give a man a fish and you feed him for a day; teach a man to fish and you feed him for a lifetime." I would also teach students how to play an instrument, because everybody needs music to lift their spirits up.

I would use my knowledge by showing others how to lead. To be a great leader, you need to get along easily with others. A great leader needs to be outspoken, but also needs to listen and hear what others have to say. I would teach others how to get along easily. In today's age, people get irritated more often, which can tend to get horrible quite quickly. I would show them how to have patience, be kind, and show respect, even when you're furious on the inside. These are basic mannerisms, but many people can lose their manners growing older.

Every day we use our knowledge and experience to help others, whether we know it or not. Also, we learn something new from somebody who has used their knowledge and experience to help us. The life of today is a give and take from each other's experience and knowledge.

Essay Example from a Student

Future Career Goals

The following essay (excerpt only) example is mostly a laundry list of activities and will probably not help this student shine in a competitive atmosphere. An essay should go further than listing activities in which a student has been involved. Answering questions that revolve around your activities such as who, what, where, how, when, and why will help to make the essay descriptive for you **and** your goals (if you relate them to your activities as shown in the *Writing Tools* section of this essay kit).

I am a student of good moral character, high academic standards, and great leadership skills. I am a senior at XYZ High School where I am ranked sixth out of my class and I have been recognized for being an honor graduate. At school I participate in many activities as well as different clubs in which I hold several leadership positions.

I am a member of FBLA, FCCLA. the Math Club in which I am the President, the Science club in which I'm the secretary and the treasurer, Student Council where I serve as Senior class treasurer, and the National Honor Society. I have been a basketball cheerleader for four years. During my tenth grade year, I was the co- captain and my eleventh and twelfth grade year I was the captain. Also, I am on the track team in which I have participated for two years.

WRITING FOR SPECIFIC ESSAY QUESTIONS

If you need to answer a specific essay question, do the following. Jot down important points you know or viewpoints you have about the subject. Do this in bullet point format. Don't waste time writing complete sentences, especially if it's a timed essay. Your answer to the question will probably be your main point, so look at the key points you wrote down and pick two or three you can develop into supporting points for two or three body paragraphs. Using the five-paragraph essay format, introduce them in the first paragraph to support your main point. Then expand on them in the body and summarize in your conclusion. As much as possible, try to relate your supporting points to your activities.

ANSWERING SHORT ESSAY QUESTIONS

For some applications you will be required to answer several questions with short essays. Short essays are usually composed of no more than one hundred words and are generally required in conjunction with a full-length essay. They are primarily concise responses to specific questions on a designated area of the application. Usually you will find these types of questions on applications for competitions consisting of several levels. Not only are these questions designed to reveal how effectively you can communicate your thoughts, but also how effectively you can communicate them in a concise and clear manner—hence the designated amount of space in which to write your short essay.

The key points to remember about responding to questions requiring short essays are to answer the questions thoroughly and to strive to keep an upbeat yet serious tone. Once you read a question, jot down possible items to include in your answer. Prioritize them and put the items that are most important at the top. Generally you will be required to answer these essay questions in the spaces allotted, so you may not be able to include everything you think of initially; hence the need for giving some items top priority. The most important concept to remember is to make statements that clearly reflect you. They should be cohesive in their entirety and also reflect a clear thought pattern.

The following is a short essay answer example. The essay was written for a scholarship competition focused on students interested in communication.

What have you accomplished in communications and English beyond regular classroom work?

In the area of communicative arts, my accomplishments have been wide and varied, mainly because my interests are broad. As captain and a member of the Academic Bowl Team, I study all subject areas for competition, especially literature.

I have maintained an "A" average in English for all my school years. I am editor-in-chief of the award-winning Salmagundi literary magazine, in which I have been published for the past four years. In 1989, I won First Prize for Best Poem in the State at the Georgia Scholastic Press Association (GSPA) competition at the University of Georgia in Athens. Writing essays for contests is a hobby of mine, and I have won Third Place for an essay on Alexander Hamilton for the Daughters of the American Revolution (DAR) and First Place for one on Sidney Lanier. In the Optimist Club Oratorical contests, I have won First Place at the zone level for the past three years and I have repeated my speeches on television. As a member of the Fine Arts and Literary Team, I have been in productions for state contests and participated in reading clubs.

THE ORGANIZER TOOLS

Organizing Your Essay

Now that you have your three adjectives, activities that go with them, and some thoughts about what to write, how do you start and organize a descriptive essay about you? Here is a basic outline of the five-paragraph format for this type of essay.

I. Introduction - One paragraph
    a. Adjective/Noun 1
    b. Adjective/Noun 2
    c. Adjective/Noun 3
II. Body - Three paragraphs
    a. Adjective/Noun 1
        i.   Activity 1
        ii. Activity 2
        iii. Activity 3
    b. Adjective/Noun 2
        i.   Activity 1
        ii. Activity 2
        iii. Activity 3
    c. Adjective/Noun 3
        i.   Activity 1
        ii. Activity 2

iii.   Activity 3

Note: You do not need to have three activities for each.

III.   Conclusion - One paragraph

     a. Summarize your adjectives and how they relate to you and your activities. Refer to the future.

For a more detailed outline to use with all types of essays, refer to the chapter, "Writing Essays That Get Noticed," in *Winning Scholarships for College*.

Based on the outline, you could begin your essay like the following example:

When I think of the words self-motivated, energetic, and compassionate, I think of myself. For the past six years, in high school and in middle school, I have participated in many activities that reflect these words. More than just words, they really describe who I am and how I feel about life.

For example in terms of self-motivation, I built a web site for students interested in getting tutors at our high school. Building the web site was a frustrating and challenging task I set for myself. It took me most of the summer before my freshman year at NE High School, but I finished it to the amazement of my parents and friends. The web site, once completed, became a much-needed reference for students in our community to find tutors to help them in all types of subjects. The web site also helped the upper-class students who became tutors make a little money to get a jump-start on college expenses. Most importantly, the site helped those who just wanted to help their peers and apply principles they learned in class and who weren't interested in charging.

As a sophomore at NE High School, I began to show more of my energetic traits by participating in several athletic activities at the same time. I joined the volleyball team. I became a varsity cheerleader…

The next paragraph would focus on compassionate. The last paragraph would be a summary and conclusion. This essay is an example of a rough draft for a descriptive essay using the adjectives self-motivated, energetic, and compassionate. It still needs work but it's meant to give you an idea of how to structure your essay using the adjectives or nouns you selected and the examples of your activities that go with them.

THE DECISION TOOLS

Deciding Your Own Topic

If you could decide your own topic for an essay, what would you write about? Browse the following topics to give you a jump-start on ideas.

- Describe yourself
- Discuss your future career goals
- Discuss an event, place, or person that has helped you grow the most
- Describe obstacles you have overcome, either physical or financial
- Discuss an event, place, or person that has had a significant impact on your life
- Describe a role model or mentor and their effect on your life
- Describe a significant move (moving from one country to another) and any major changes it has brought about in your life
- Discuss how a death in your family has affected you
- Describe your plans for while you're in college (i.e. study abroad,

independent research or study, in-depth study of a foreign language, internship, cooperative education)

- Discuss what you are doing now and what you plan to do in the future for your community
- In your essay, you could also answer the following questions as a topic.
  - o If you're at your tenth, twentieth, or thirtieth high school reunion, what you would like to have achieved?
  - o What has been your biggest failure and what did you learn?
  - o What is your greatest achievement and what did you learn?

OUTLINE TOOLS

Deciding Your Own Topic

You can use the following outline examples for some of the topics in the Decision Tools section.

Outline Example 1

I. What is your most outstanding accomplishment? (first paragraph)
   a. Describe the accomplishment.
   b. Why did you decide to get started or involved?
   c. When did the accomplishment occur?
   d. Where did the accomplishment occur?
   e. Who did the accomplishment involve other than yourself?
II. How did you achieve the accomplishment? (second paragraph)
III. How do you think this achievement changed you or will change you? (third paragraph)

IV.   Did you or do you expect to help someone else in the process? (fourth paragraph)

V.   Where has this accomplishment led you? (fifth paragraph)

For all paragraphs, consider the questions: Who? What? Where? When? How? Why?

Outline Example 2

I.   Describe a situation or problem in your community, school, or another area. State your solution as the main idea. (first paragraph)

II.   Why does or will your solution work? (second paragraph)

III.   How did or will you accomplish your solution? (third paragraph)

IV.   Who does or will your solution help? (fourth paragraph)

V.   What is or will be the future situation after your solution was/is implemented (results)? (fifth paragraph)

TYPICAL ESSAY PROMPTS

For Scholarship Applications From Private Organizations

1. Provide a personal statement. A personal statement is basically a description of yourself, your activities, and your goals.

2. Whom do you admire and respect the most? Why?

3. What activity or program is most meaningful to you? What are your reason(s) for getting involved?

4. What is the most interesting and profound book that you have read recently? Why?

5. What is the worst crisis or problem facing Americans today?

6. Describe your most challenging achievement, how you accomplished it, the obstacles you faced, and its impact on your life?

7. Why should you receive this scholarship or award?
8. Tell us about an extracurricular or volunteer activity that has had the most meaning to you and why?
9. What are your future career goals?

For College/University Applications

1. Why do you want to attend this university or college?
2. Discuss a political, social, or economic issue that is important to you.
3. Comment on a recent scientific or technological advance and the impact it may have on the future.
4. Why did you choose _____for a future career choice?
5. Describe your ideal teacher.
6. What is the best advice you have received and why?
7. What characteristics do you have that would contribute to this college or university?

ESSAY REVIEW TOOLS

Use the following questions as a checklist to review your essay and perfect it.

1. Is your writing truthful and accurate?

2. Did you proofread your printed essay at least three times very carefully? **<u>Do not proofread exclusively on the computer. Print your essay to thoroughly proofread and avoid mistakes!</u>**

3. Have you asked someone else to read it?

4. Is your essay neatly presented? (Double-spaced, printed on white paper of good quality, etc.)

5. Did you thoroughly respond to the essay question?

6. Do all the supporting paragraphs contribute to the overall theme of your essay?

7. Have you conveyed your enthusiasm in the presentation of your opinions and ideas?

8. Did you incorporate information about your extracurricular and

community service activities in your essay?

9. Did you refer to the future in terms of how you will contribute to the campus of a particular university or college, your community, or society overall?

10. Did you use transition words? A list of transition words is available at the end of this chapter. Peruse the example essays to see how transition words can be used to make your written words more cohesive.

11. Use a thesaurus and a dictionary for word variety and appropriate word choice.

12. Help your reader to visualize your subject by using descriptive words and phrases.

13. Show your feelings (positive only, please) about your activities.

14. Don't go over the word limit.

TOOLS FOR USING TRANSITION WORDS

Use any of the following words to help make your essay more cohesive. They can also help you to establish a flow between your thoughts, words, sentences, and paragraphs.

TRANSITION WORDS that can be used to **contrast** two things *(you might use one of these when you explain your participation in one activity and another dissimilar activity)*:

- *still*
- *although*
- *on the other hand*
- *however*
- *yet*
- *otherwise*
- *even though*

TRANSITION WORDS that can be used to **compare** two things *(you might use one of these when you explain your participation in one activity and another similar or dissimilar activity)*:

- *likewise*
- *also*
- *while*
- *in the same way*
- *as*
- *similarly*

TRANSITION WORDS that can be used to **emphasize a point in your essay** *(you might use one of these to emphasize why an extracurricular activity is so important to you)*:
- *again*
- *truly*
- *especially*
- *for this reason*
- *to repeat*
- *in fact*
- *to emphasize*

TRANSITION WORDS that can be used to **conclude or summarize** *(you might use one of these in your last paragraph)*:
- *finally*
- *as a result*
- *to sum up*

- *in conclusion*
- *lastly*
- *therefore*
- *all in all*
- *because*

TRANSITION WORDS that can be used to **add information** *(you may need these if you are discussing more than one event or activity in your essay)*:

- *again*
- *another*
- *also*
- *and*
- *along with*
- *other*
- *next*
- *additionally*
- *for example*
- *for instance*
- *finally*
- *in addition*
- *furthermore*

- *moreover*
- *as well*
- *besides*

TRANSITION WORDS that can be used to **explain further or clarify**:

- *that is*
- *for instance*
- *in other words*
- *as stated previously*

TRANSITION WORDS that can be used to show **time** *(you might use these when explaining when you participated in certain activities)*:

- *while*
- *first*
- *meanwhile*
- *soon*
- *then*
- *after*
- *second*
- *today*
- *later*
- *next*
- *at*
- *third*
- *tomorrow*
- *afterward*
- *as soon as*
- *before*
- *now*
- *yesterday*
- *about*
- *during*
- *until*
- *throughout*
- *finally*

TOOLS FOR GETTING YOUR ESSAY NOTICED

Here are a few items to help you write the best essays and stand out from the crowd.

1.   Answer the question.

2.   When you're writing an essay, it's easy to ramble. When you finish your first draft, go back and reread the question to make sure you've answered it.

3.   Do not give a laundry list of activities but make sure you write about them!

4.   An essay is where you can really shine and tell those who read the essay how you feel about a particular activity. In fact, incorporating your activities, how they have helped to make you into the student or person you are, and how those activities may have helped others, are important features to include in an essay and make its content come alive for the readers. Always try to answer these questions when writing about an activity:

•   What is the activity and why are you involved?

•   Who does the activity benefit?

- How does this activity benefit you or others?

5. Proofread! Proofread! Proofread!

6. Typos and spelling or grammatical errors will not make a good first impression. Don't rely on your computer's spell check. Reread your essays several times; then ask someone else to read your essays for errors as well.

7. If applicable, include your answers to these questions in your essay.

- Have you faced any challenges?
- Have you overcome obstacles or hardships?
- What makes you unique? For example, a girl on a high school football team would be different.
- Have your achievements had an incredible impact on others or yourself?
- Have you significantly changed your life in some way? For example, you transformed from an extremely poor student to a great student.

- How has your commitment and service to others changed your life or that of another person?

FINAL ESSAY THOUGHTS

- Complete your résumé/activity list before you begin your essay.
- Research the organization that sponsors the scholarship or award you are trying to win. Know their purpose and mission. Know why the scholarship or award was established.
- Use a thesaurus and a dictionary.
- Write a rough draft. It's important to get ideas down on paper, rather than wasting time worrying about punctuation, grammar, and making it pretty before you have a whole essay.
- Be unique. What is different about your experiences and activities than any other applicant? Highlight these differences.
- Help your reader to visualize your subject.
- Focus on your activities.
- Show your feelings (positive only, please) about your activities.
- For all of your activities you should think about the following:
  - How did you contribute?

- o How did the activity help you or others?
  - o What is the activity preparing you for?
- Don't go over the word limit.
- Spell check.
- Proofread and then get someone else to proofread.
- Edit, edit, and edit!
- Support your main point with each paragraph.
- Answer the essay question. Don't ramble.
- Make your essay original and thought provoking.
- Be specific and detailed. Answer who, what, when, where, and how, when writing about your activities.
- Writing many essays can take time. Don't be afraid to recycle portions of previous essays when applying for multiple scholarships.

RESOURCE TOOLS

Other Essay Resources

On-line Resources

- Essay Writing Webinars with Marianne Ragins
  - o www.scholarshipworkshop.com

- Merriam-Webster Dictionary
  - o www.m-w.com/dictionary

- Grammarly
  - o www.grammarly.com

- The Blue Book of Grammar and Punctuation
  - o www.grammarbook.com

- Paradigm Online Writing Assistant
  - o www.powa.org

- Quoteland.com
  - o www.quoteland.com

- Strunk and White's Elements of Style

- www.bartleby.com/141/index.ht
  ml

Off-line Resources

- *Webster's II: New College Dictionary*
- *Roget's Super Thesaurus* by Marc
  McCutcheon

APPENDIX

Other Resources from Marianne Ragins

Books and Publications

The Scholarship & College Essay Planning Kit
- If you have trouble getting beyond a blank page when it comes to writing an essay, this resource is for you. This resource is updated yearly.

Get Money for College – An Audio Series
- If you don't have time to read a book or attend a class but you do have time to listen, this audio series can help you learn how to find and win scholarships for college.

10 Steps for Using the Internet in Your Scholarship Search
- This is a resource designed to be used at your computer to walk you step by step through using the Internet for your scholarship search. It keeps you from being overwhelmed by the massive amount of sometimes misleading

information found on the web. This
resource is updated yearly.

The Scholarship Monthly Planning Calendar
- This convenient and easy to use
  monthly planning calendar will help
  you with time management, getting
  organized, and staying on track with
  activities to meet major scholarship and
  award deadlines. This resource is
  updated yearly.

Winning Scholarships for College
- In *Winning Scholarships for College*,
  Marianne Ragins, the winner of more
  than $400,000 in scholarship funds,
  proves that it`s not always the students
  with the best grades or the highest SAT
  scores who win scholarships. Whether
  you are in high school, returning to or
  currently enrolled in college, or
  planning to study abroad, this easy to
  follow college scholarship guide will
  show you the path to scholarship
  success. One of the most comprehensive
  books on winning scholarships and
  written by a successful scholarship
  recipient, it reveals where and how to

search for funds, and walks you step by step through the scholarship application process.

Last Minute College Financing Guide
- If you've got the acceptance letter, but are still wondering how to pay the tuition bill because you haven't yet started searching for college money, this resource is for you!

Workshops & Boot Camps

The Scholarship Workshop Presentation
- In The Scholarship Workshop presentation which is a 1, 2, or 3 hour interactive seminar, speaker Marianne Ragins proves that it is not always the student with the best grades or the highest SAT scores who wins scholarships. Instead she shows students of all ages that most scholarships are awarded to students who exhibit the best preparation. By attending The Scholarship Workshop presentation, a student will be well prepared to meet the challenge of finding and winning scholarships. The presentation is designed to help

students conduct a successful scholarship search from the research involved in finding scholarship money to the scholarship essays, scholarship interview tips and strategies involved in winning them. This presentation is usually sponsored by various organizations and individuals usually attend at no cost. Attendees of the presentation become eligible for the Ragins/Braswell National scholarship sponsored by Marianne. If you or your organization is interested in sponsoring a workshop or motivational presentation with Marianne Ragins, visit www.scholarshipworkshop.com.

The Scholarship Workshop Weekend Boot Camp

- This is an expanded version of The Scholarship Workshop presentation – It is a full day and a half of activities designed to help students and parents leave the weekend with scholarship essays, résumés, and applications completed and ready to go. The workshop weekend boot camp is usually sponsored by various organizations and individuals usually attend at no cost. Attendees of the presentation become eligible for the Ragins/Braswell National scholarship sponsored by Marianne. If you or your organization is interested in sponsoring a workshop or motivational presentation with Marianne Ragins, visit www.scholarshipworkshop.com.

Webinars & Online Classes

- *The Scholarship Class for High School Students and Their Parents*

- *Scholarship, Fellowship & Grant Information Session for Students Already in College, Returning to College, and Pursuing Graduate School*
    - The above classes are webinar versions of the Scholarship Workshop presentation. It is offered for those who do not live in an area where a workshop is being sponsored. Attendees of either class become eligible for the Ragins/Braswell National Scholarship.

- *Writing Scholarship & College Essays for the Uneasy Student Writer* – A Webinar

- *Turbocharge Your Résumé - Résumé Writing Skills to Help You Stand Out from the Crowd* – A Webinar

- *Preparation Skills for Scholarship & College Interviews* – A Webinar

- *Minimizing College Costs and Student Loans* – A Webinar

For more information about webinars and online classes available, visit www.scholarshipworkshop.com/online-classes.

eBooks

Marianne Ragins also has numerous e-Books available for Nook, Kindle and iPad. Visit www.scholarshipworkshop.com/ebooks for the latest!

You can find information and additional resources from Marianne Ragins by visiting or connecting with her using the following:
- www.scholarshipworkshop.com

- www.facebook.com/scholarshipworkshop
- www.twitter.com/ScholarshipWork
- www.shop.scholarshipworkshop.com

ABOUT THE AUTHOR

In her senior year of high school, Marianne Ragins won over $400,000 in scholarships for college. As perhaps the first student ever to amass nearly half a million dollars in scholarship money, she has been featured in many publications including *USA Today, People, Ebony, Newsweek, Money, Essence, Family Money, Black Enterprise* and on the cover of *Parade*. She has also made hundreds of radio and television appearances on shows such as "Good Morning America," "The Home Show," and the "Mike & Maty Show."

Marianne Ragins received a master of business administration (MBA) from George Washington University in Washington, DC and a bachelor of science (BS) degree in business administration from Florida Agricultural and Mechanical University in Tallahassee, Florida. Both degrees were entirely funded by scholarships and other free aid.

Marianne Ragins is also the author of the highly successful *Winning Scholarships for College: An Insider's Guide* and many other publications. She is an experienced motivational speaker and lecturer who has traveled nationally and internationally conducting The Scholarship Workshop presentation and giving other motivational seminars and speeches. Marianne is the publisher of www.scholarshipworkshop.com, a scholarship and college information site, and sponsor of the *Leading the Future II* and *Ragins Braswell National Scholarships*.

Contact Marianne Ragins using any of the following sources:
- www.scholarshipworkshop.com
- www.facebook.com/scholarshipworkshop
- www.twitter.com/ScholarshipWork

Made in the USA
Middletown, DE
19 October 2024